About the author

I am quite an ordinary bloke, with nothing exceptional about me other than my ability to connect with the numinous, or if you prefer, the Divine.

Some would say I am a mystic, but if I am, then so are you, as we are *all* connected to the Divine. In truth, we are all Divine Beings—we are all Living Gods.

You, I, and all the 7.8 billion other people on Planet Earth, possess God consciousness; we possess this consciousness by virtue of our Soul—which is a part of God.

Original artwork by Lynn De Lacey www.artzafari.com

By the same author

God as Avatar

Relationships

Letters to my Child

The Way: A Penetrating Insight into the Mysteries of Life

LIFE'S LITTLE BOOK OF SAYINGS

Bazza

LIFE'S LITTLE BOOK OF SAYINGS

Vanguard Press

VANGUARD PAPERBACK

A CIP catalogue record for this title is
available from the British Library.

ISBN 9781800161023

*Vanguard Press is an imprint of
Pegasus Elliot MacKenzie Publishers Ltd.*
www.pegasuspublishers.com

First Published in 2022

**Vanguard Press
Sheraton House Castle Park
Cambridge England**

Printed & Bound in Great Britain

LIFE'S LITTLE BOOK OF SAYINGS
BOOK 1

The contents of this little booklet have been derived from the material presented in Bazza's seminal book, *Relationships – The Spiritual and the Profane.*

Whilst each saying represents a stand-alone statement; collectively, the overall theme of them all is to encourage *you* to reclaim your God-given power of self-determination.

Saying 64 declares that: "The Unseen Hand will guide you; unasked; to your destiny."

It may well be that the *Unseen Hand* has guided you to this very book!

Knowledge is what you have

Wisdom is what you are

Wisdom is knowledge made manifest.

Life will continually strive to challenge you.
It will do this by throwing obstacles
across your path,
some large - some small.

Each one, large and small, is pregnant
with opportunity;
the small ones are no less important
than the large.

To ignore the small, is to miss an even larger
opportunity for growth.

The secret is in discerning which one
to focus on.

Time is relative.

Being relative
it can only exist in a physical world
such as Planet Earth.

Time is a measurement.
It is a measurement between
this and that.

Cosmic "time" is absolute.
It exists only in non-physical realms
such as the Spirit World.

In such realms,
past, present, and future all co-exist,
so all measurements become meaningless.

Beware the enslavement of time.

*In seeking to be healed, choose
your healer carefully.*

*Neither you, nor your healer,
are independent of each other.*

*Each of you contributes something to the
healing process.*

*In truth, it is ultimately YOU, who is the
miracle worker.*

Not the healer!

In Life, there are no right or wrong paths.

There are only *different paths.*

If the path you are on
is not taking you where you want to be,
then choose another path.

How can you tell what is the "right" path?

If you encounter a problem once - take note.

If you encounter the same problem
twice - be alert.

If it happens for a third time -
a pattern is sealed.

All living things are dependent upon the
Elemental Kingdom; which is a composition of
the four elements:
Fire - Water - Earth - Air.

Plants, belonging to the Nature Kingdom, are
dependent on the four elements for their
sustenance and growth.

Man cannot survive without plants.
Even the carnivorous animals
Man kills to eat
have derived their energy source
from plants;
the plants at the beginning of the
food chain.
Man's survival is also heavily dependent on
fossil fuels:
fuels that initially derived from plants.

How is it, then, that Man has so little regard
for the Elemental and Nature Kingdoms?

Teach without words.

Work without doing.

This is the way of Nature.
This is living in the NOW.

To fully understand Nature

you must become One with the object
of your Desire.

This process of merging leads to the gateway of
Universal Wisdom:

Here, all you need to know will be revealed.

*Health is subject to the Laws of Creation
and Karma.*

*You create every condition that relates to
your health.*

*If you are dissatisfied with your health
it is you that needs to change - to create a
new you.*

*Karma neither punishes, nor rewards.
It simply allows you to experience what you
have already created!*

Man is a pack animal. Man is tribal.

Man is a group animal.

Yet unlike other grouping species,
Man is reluctant to share any
new knowledge.
Man keeps that knowledge for personal gain.

All other species immediately share their
knowledge and thus survive.

In the absence of change
Man will surely perish.

*Seek no external validation.
Seek only from within.*

*How can another validate you
when they do not even know
who they themselves are?*

*Those who are spiritually aware
would never judge another.*

When in doubt, ask your Self
what would Love do now?
What would the Sage do now?

Whenever in doubt, go within.
For there, both Love and the Sage dwell.

Ask, and it shall be revealed.

I do not compete
so I do not meet with competition.
I do not argue,
so I have no one to argue with.
I do not judge,
So I am immune to judgement.

I am sufficient unto my Self.

*All personal behaviour
is a declaration of who you are.
It is an act of Self Revelation
You are revealing to the world – this is
who I Am*

*Be wary therefore of what you put on display
For what others can see, you may not.*

Peace and Freedom are mutually supportive.
Each is reliant upon the other

To be free, is to release all attachments, and
all addictions

How can you be free, if you are attached
to something?

And until you are *totally* Free
Peace will forever elude you.

Nothing matters beyond the
Present Moment

Only in that Present Moment did it matter
and then only to the degree that your Life has
been affected.

From that moment on you have a new Life
It is how you *choose* to live your new Life
that will determine your future.

*The single most important issue facing
humanity today
is a critical lack of Self-empowerment
and Self-determination*

We are drowning in a sea of external controls

*Self-empowerment grows out of genuine and
heart-felt Self-Love.*

*Self-Love can move mountains
It will create miracles, and collectively, it can
and will change the world.*

If attacked, a tree of the forest can neither
run away nor fight back
It has no defence against the destructive
onslaught of Man

Yet paradoxically, it is the tree that will
ultimately be the survivor
Man will perish, for want of what the tree
provided.

To live in fear of another, is to give your power
to the other.

All fears are born of imaginings.

You are no less powerful than another.

True power comes from within.

There is no power on earth strong enough to
break your Eternal Spirit.

Beware your Shadow Self

*Within its deepest and darkest layers reside
the potential for all manner of evil.*

*Also within, resides the potential for your
highest good.*

*Good and evil, are naught but the light and
dark of each other.*

In choosing, you are choosing your Life.

Choose well!

In communication be direct,
yet remain open.

In action, balance strength with fairness.

In this way, all outcomes will be rewarded.

Allow Purity of Heart, and Purity of Thought,
to be your guiding principles.

Loneliness is a state of separation.
Aloneness is a state of Oneness

One can be alone, yet not feel lonely
and one can be lonely, yet not be alone.

Aloneness is a state of Being.
Loneliness is a state of Mind.

Love gives all, and requires nothing.
If something is required,
it is not True Love .

Love gives to all.
Love does not discriminate.

Can a golden sunset give its beauty to one
and not to the other?

Can a Love-infused heart
give and withhold at the same time?
I do not believe so.

God IS Love. God gives Love to All.

There is perfection in every person.
There is perfection in all sentient Beings.

What appears to be imperfect is only
an illusion.

The illusion created by incompleteness.

God does not create imperfection.

Our state of incompleteness is a state
of opportunity:
an opportunity for us to grow
an opportunity to reach our full potential for
wholeness.

This is God's Way.

Growth begins
at the end of your comfort zone.
No pain - no gain.

All adversity is a gift from the Universe.
It is the gift of opportunity.

All dark clouds have a silver lining
and within the darkness
lies the seed of Light.

Find your seed and nurture it.
Nurture it with all the Love
that you possess.

*There are too many adult people walking
Planet Earth
with a frightened child hiding within.*

What is birth?
It is the prelude to death.

What is death?
It is the prelude to Life.

This is the eternal cycle and rhythm of Life.
It is the Life-cycle of your Soul.

Embrace each; both birth and death,
with anticipation, gusto, and Love.

Fear not.

There is enough.

There is always enough

and in all ways, there is enough.

*In all relational situations,
the question to be asked is:
What do I want for this relationship?
Not - what does the other want?*

*You are never responsible for another
nor are they ever responsible for you.
Each has to take full responsibility for
their actions.*

*In this way each can grow to their
highest potential.*

Nothing in the Universe happens by accident -
there are NO accidents.

In creating the Universe, God did not make
any mistakes.

Everything has been planned for since the
beginning of Time.

All mystery will disappear, once you realise
that your Soul had planned your Life
in advance.

Once embodied in a physical body,
you were denied all memory of your
new Life's plan.
How your new Life unfolds then becomes
dependant on the choices you make
along the way.

It is the choices that you do make, that will
define you as a person.

*In the same way as God created the
Grand Universe
so do you create your own
Personal Universe.*

*All people, and all events,
whether you experience them either as good or
bad - you have created!*

*If you are unhappy with your present Life,
create a new Life.*

*If you are unhappy with the people
around you,
re-create them anew.*

*All of Life is but an illusion, an illusion
created by your Self.*

*You have the God-given creative power to
create whatever you choose - even God!*

*In times of crisis
the most powerful expression of Love
that you can give to another
is to either leave them be
or empower them to help themselves.*

*Give nothing that disempowers – give only
what empowers.*

*Sometimes
to do nothing is more empowering
than uninvited intervention.*

*Prior to giving
let the other know what it is you have to give.
It may be they are not yet ready, or willing, to
receive it.*

God is genderless.

An eternity of Man's wailing and gnashing
of teeth
will never turn God into a male.

An eternity of protestations and cries of heresy
from all the religions of the world
will never turn God into a male.

To imagine that God, the Supreme Creator,
Would, as an after-thought,
create woman from the rib of man
is either gross male arrogance, sheer insanity,
or both!

God is neither Father, nor Mother.
God is both Father and Mother.
God is - God.

Whenever I am *not awake,*
I choose to sleep.

I find this preferable to wandering around in
a fog of unknowing

and aimlessly filling in the time between birth
and death.

*If you aspire to understand another
it is necessary to enter their world.*

*Equally, for you to be understood
by the other
they need an understanding
of your world.*

*In the absence of these mutual
understandings
all meaningful communication is lost.*

Is there a hell?
Yes there is.

Where is hell?
It is in the minds of those
who have separated from their Soul.

To lose contact with your Soul
is to experience a living hell on Earth.

Your Soul-Self has joined with your
physical body
to enact a Life of growth-enhancing
achievements.

It is when your Body-Self splits
or fractures the relationship with your
Soul-Self
that you will indeed experience
a Life of hell.

To exit hell, go on a quest to re-discover your
true Self

And, once found, become as One with your
Soul-Self.

*There is nowhere to go,
as you are already there.*

*The path leading to Eternal Truth is endless.
It is a journey to nowhere*

*You are always where
you have chosen to Be.*

*In choosing to follow another path
always follow your heart.*

Everyone has a gift for humanity.

There are no greater or lesser Beings.

Those called great, are ordinary people doing
great things.
They are sharing their gift with humanity.

Sadly, the smaller gifts go largely unnoticed
yet each small gift is as important as the
great gift.

Collectively, the smaller gifts have an even
greater impact on the overall wellbeing
of humanity.

Is selfishness a virtue, or a curse?

Selfishness is the passionate pursuit to
accomplish a chosen desire
and in the face of all resistance.

If the desire is for the benefit of humanity
selfishness is indeed virtuous.

If the desire is for the benefit of the instigator
to the exclusion of others, it becomes a curse.
Jesus practiced selfishness to perfection: as did
Mother Theresa.

As with all things in Life, choice of intent
becomes the deciding factor.

Reality is an in-the-moment
sensory experience.

The experience is real, it is palpable, and
it is happening.
Plus, it is happening NOW.

All else is but an illusion.
It is a self-created fantasy of an imaginary,
yet unreal future.

All things illusionary have no substance.
They are not REAL.

*Is it possible to experience
Heaven on Earth?*

Yes – it is.

*You experience Heaven on Earth whenever you
are at peace with your Self.*

*The moment you achieve inner-peace, you are
at peace with the whole world.*

This is the desire of your Soul.

*Once at peace with the world, you are at peace
with all that lives on Earth.*

*You will experience all those around you in a
joyful way.
You will appreciate the beauty and wonder of
all that nature has to offer.
You will know that this is what God has
intended for you.*

This is Heaven on Earth.

*The widening gulf between those who are
spiritually aware
and those who are living in a barren state of
spiritual unconsciousness
is a matter of grave concern for the future
wellbeing of humanity.*

*This gulf has an inverse correlation to the
material world of haves and have-nots.*

*The have-nots are more spiritually aware
whilst the haves are lost in a fog of their
own making.*

Souls are genderless.

Whilst still at home in the spirit world,
your Soul
will choose a body type, personality,
and sex
that will support its new Life to be.

The choice it makes will depend on the type
of experiences
it wishes to have during the course of its
new Life.

The choice of gender is rarely a consideration
in making this choice.

A gift is not a gift

if it requires something in return.

Is Man the only species in the Universe with
intelligence? No, he is not.

Is Man the only species on Earth with
intelligence? No, he is not.

Is Man of superior intelligence to woman? No,
he is not.

Is Man the most highly evolved species on the
planet? No, he is not.

Man's delusion is driven by fear - fear of not
being any of these things.

In desperation, Man tries to maintain
his delusion
by either destroying, or controlling, that
which he fears.

Man is a danger to himself, and ultimately, to
the planet.

Man seems hell-bent on destroying everyone
and everything
that stands in the way of his insatiable greed
- especially the world of Nature.

If Man does not wipe himself out through some
monstrous conflagration
he will certainly do so by destroying the very
thing that ensures his survival:
our natural environment.

In the absence of radical and
fundamental change
it will be a race to the bottom to see what
calamity takes us out first.

The Power of One has multiple layers
of meaning

God, with all the power to have created the
Universe, is The One.

To be At One with another
is the power that results from the merging with
another

If only the *strong* could recognise the truth in
the saying
"the whole is greater than the sum
of its parts"

The *strong* fear being pulled back by
the *weak*
when in reality the opposite is true

Once joined, the energy of the weak
adds power to the energy of the strong

Thus is created the Power of One.

You have nothing to Do.

You have only to Be.

Our world is over-populated by mannequins.

Mannequins who parade the world stage as
though in a masquerade party.

They are not real people: They are
self-styled actors,
each believing in the lie of their own
performance.

Every layer of society is afflicted by them,
all the way to the highest of high
in both governments and
religious institutions.

The tragedy is
their performance can be so convincing
that their followers believe in them.

This situation will remain so unless,
and until,
the same people who are blinded by their
performance
can see through the charade and reclaim
their own
God-given power.

Forgiveness is a Divine Paradox.

On the one hand it releases the perpetrator.
On the other, it entraps the aggrieved.

Through the act of forgiveness,
the aggrieved is declaring that
they are a victim.

At a Soul level, all events have been planned
for; consequently there are no victims, and
no villains.

Each Soul is experiencing that which had been
planned for

So there is nothing to forgive, as there is
nobody to forgive.

Each has the opportunity to grow from their
own individual experience.

The length of time you may live on Planet
Earth is of little importance.

What is important
is how you have lived your Life
in that same time.

Is your Life's mission complete?
Have you fulfilled your purpose in Life?
On reflection, are you satisfied with how your
Life has turned out?

To fill your time between birth and death
and waiting and hoping for a better
tomorrow is to waste a precious
God-given Life.

Live each day as though it were your last!

I am what I create - I create what I am.

I Am, and Creation are One.

Love is the beginning and end of
The Universe.
Love is the centre of The Universe.
Love Is The Universe.

Your heart is the centre of Your Universe.
Whenever confusion arises, ask - what would
Love do now?

There is no meaning to Life.
Yet sometimes there is purpose to Life
and occasionally,
there is no purpose to Life
Life - just Is.

Paradoxically,
there can be meaning to Life.

It is to be found in everything that you do, or
not do
and the manner in which you respond to
Life's events.

All responses are Self-defining.

Only by going Within

will you discover

there is no Without.

Love of Self is synonymous with Love of God.

*If you are unable to Love your Self, how can
you Love another?*

Love and God are inseparable.

*God created all Beings, including You,
out of Love.*

God IS Love.

Intent - within this one word dwells the power
of the Universe.

Intent is charged with a force that can move
mountains.

It can create an energy force so powerful
that miracles can, and do, happen.

Unfortunately - this same energy force
can be used for ill-intent.

Fortunately - Karma will exact a price from
those who abuse this force.

*Society is suffering from an insidious malaise;
a serious lack of Self-worth*

*It permeates all strata of society;
sapping our essential Life-force.*

*Because we feel powerless, we transfer our
power to others.*

*We feel powerless because we have given away
our power
to those whom we believe are superior to us.*

It is not too late – reclaim your power!

There are Souls who incarnate as a Messiah.
There are Souls who incarnate as a Prophet.

Then, there are Souls who incarnate as
a Sage.

The Messiah and the Prophet will touch the
lives of many.

The Sage will touch the lives of a few.

It matters not what clothes these great
Masters wear
nor whom their messages touch.

All are messengers of God.
All have the same message - clothed in
different language.

Life is a process

And the process is in the present moment.
The present moment is all there IS.

The past is naught but an ancient relic,
something for you to occasionally
reflect upon.

As for the future,
it can never be more than a
pregnant mystery.

What does it mean "go with the flow?"

It means that Life's inevitable progression
is relentless.

Life does not compromise.
Life does not punish.
Life does not reward.

Life just - IS.

Life goes on - with or without you.
So you may as well hop on board and go with
the flow!

Knowledge is Power.

It is for this reason, religions and governments
do not want you to be educated - in Life!

They only want to teach dogma, maths
and science.

In this way you become educated enough to
oil their machines of control.

Thus, they have turned you into one of
their slaves.

You have been brainwashed to believe that
you are helpless and insignificant.
Thus you need to be subservient to them at
all times
and in all ways.

Lessons in Life - lessons in Spirituality,
lessons given to Empower you are forbidden.

Break free - Teach your Self - Empower
your Self.

*Living a Life by choice
is living a Life by Creative and
Conscious Action.*

*Living a Life by chance
is living a Life of Unconscious Reaction.*

*Present experience
is your only guide to living a creative and
healthy Life.*

What is the difference between religion and
spirituality? The religionists would have you
believe there is no difference

There is a difference; the difference is that
religion teaches the will of God
and the law of God.

God does not have a will for us; God has
preferences, yet will never enforce those
preferences. God cares for us, as any loving
parent would, yet will never intervene. God
has blessed us with free-will to do as we please.
God will neither prevent us, nor rescue us if we
stumble

Jesus was a child of God

Jesus incarnated into the Jewish faith
to challenge its religious practices

Jesus did not come to establish a new religion
He came to clean up the existing one, and
return it to spirituality

Jesus did not write any new laws
He taught by example - by His actions.

*The Unseen Hand will guide you - unasked -
to your Destiny.*

*What does it mean
to be Empty and Still?*

*To be Empty
means you have discarded
everything superfluous,
all the things that have cluttered your Life.*

*To be Still
means you are centred and grounded.
You do not move far from the Centre.*

The ground of our existence guides the quality
of our lives.

Rising out of this ground are the agents
for conflict.
Rising out of this ground are the agents
for peace.

These agents are active at both the personal
and global level.

The perception of a smooth ground surface
will promote peace and harmony.
The perception of a rough surface will
engender conflict and disharmony.

The ground of your existence is relative to
your internal state of Being.

Your internal state of Being
colours your perception of all things.

The lure of the Forbidden.

What is it about the Forbidden
that draws us into its vortex?

Perhaps it is the promise of adventure.
Perhaps it is the thrill of taking a risk.
Perhaps it is a need to live on the edge.

Whatever it is: for me, it remains a mystery.

In any meaningful communication
with another
it is wise to be mindful of what is not
being said.

Also, to be alert to any incongruent or
absent behaviour.

What is not being said, and what is not
being done,
are equally as important as what is being said
and done.

Conflict, at both a personal and societal level,
has its genesis in misplaced and out of
sync desires.

These misplaced and out of sync desires,
in turn, are birthed by
unrealistic expectations.

At a personal level
the conflict is between the separate parts
of Self.

At a societal level
it is among the peoples of all nations.

Those who are unwilling to accept others'
differences.

*The world of Man
is governed by Fear and Greed,
two very powerful emotions.*

*In the mind of Man
fear and greed reign supreme
over an even greater emotion - Love.*

*In an ideal world
Love would be the only governing emotion.*

*Unfortunately, we do not live in an
ideal world.*

We are all three part Beings.

Your first part
is the body that your Soul chose for its
physical Life.

Your second part
is that which has been created
through the merging of your body and Soul.
This is your Body-Self.

Your third part
represents the Eternal Soul.
This is your Soul-Self.

Any fracture or separation of your
Body-Self from your Soul-Self
will create disharmony at best
or a breakdown of physical and mental
health at worst.

If your Life is in disarray
go within and seek counsel from your
Higher Self.

History teaches
that Man has been in a state of war
since the rise of Homo Sapiens.

Is Man destined to be so for all eternity?

History also teaches that Man is capable of
profound acts of Love.

Can these two polarities be reconciled?

All wars are fuelled by Fear:

Fear of losing control;
Fear of not having enough;
Fear of losing what you have;
Fear of others having more or better than you.

Fear is an absence of Love
Fear cannot exist in the presence of Love.

A life well lived, is a Life filled with virtue.

A Life lived well, is a Life inspired by virtue.

What is a virtue?

A virtue is any thought or act that is uplifting
for humanity.

The most time-honoured virtues are:

compassion, tolerance, acceptance, patience,
forgiveness, empathy, honesty and charity.

To be giving of your Self with any of
these qualities
is the greatest gift that you could give
to humanity.

*What you most despise in others
is a hidden and unacknowledged part of
your Self.*

Thought begets action.

Action begets experience.

Experience begets embodiment.

Embodiment begets wisdom.

Wisdom begets the "I Am".
From the "I Am" arises thought.

Humanity is in dire need of something to pull
it out of its death dive.
That something may well be the raising of our
Collective Consciousness,

Consciousness raised into a state of virtuous
thought and behaviour.

To understand this, one only has to observe a
colony of ants or bees:
They all behave as a single unit

Similarly, to watch a flock of birds, or a school
of fish:
They all turn in precise union.

They are all behaving for the collective good
of the whole.

What the world needs now
is a collective consciousness that
is philanthropic
and all-embracing.

We are all One.

Man is living the greatest lie of the Universe.

Man believes he is Lord over all things.

Man is Lord of only his fears.

*Suicide is a viable option for your Soul;
yet only when your body can no longer
sustain a Life with dignity.*

*Suicide, whilst still with a physically and
mentally healthy body, is not an option.*

*Souls who choose to exit a healthy body
will be sent back to complete their previously
planned-for Life agenda.*

*Souls choose the Life they most need
to experience.*

One should never attempt to
"push the river"
as all you get is wet hands.

All of Life's events
will only reveal themselves when their
time has come

and not one second sooner!

Life and Mystery are One.

Each dwells within the other,

Mystery within Mystery.

The centre of a wheel does not wobble.

The centre of a wheel does not wear out.

Keep therefore to the centre.

You Are what you believe in.

Your beliefs form the foundation of
"This is who I Am".

Your I Am then becomes a statement
of who you Are.

This cycle cannot be broken, unless, and until,
you make a choice to step outside of it.

In stepping outside, you are then free:
free to create a new I Am.

Anticipation, as with expectation, can be a dangerous drug.

The present moment may indeed be pregnant with anticipation.

However, delivery may not be forthcoming!

Freedom can easily become entrapment!

In the pursuit of freedom
you may have to release one principle
so as to embrace the other.

True freedom can only be realised by the
release of all principles.

*Dependence engenders feelings of
weakness, vulnerability and powerlessness.*

*You have the power, and the ability,
to achieve whatever you so desire.*

At all times, be sufficient unto your Self.

Life just IS.

IS-ness cannot be explained.

It follows no logic: it is both illogical
and paradoxical.

IS-ness, exists and disappears in the
same instant.

You cannot see it, hold it, contain it, nor
capture it.

IS-ness is the Alpha and the Omega

Life just IS.

*To behold a golden sunset
is worth more than all the treasures on Earth.*

*To witness such a spectacle
is to witness the magnificence of God
in action.*

*The sunset is a beautiful metaphor
for the passing of your mortal Self
to yet another beautiful realm of existence.*

*In the same way
a glorious sunrise is heralding in the promise
of a new Life.*

Planning for death should begin at birth.

This - is all there IS.

Until - it is NOT.

MY PRAYER FOR YOU

I LOVE YOU - these are the words that I want you to carry with you, in your heart of hearts, for all eternity.

I LOVE YOU, and in loving you, I become you; you and I, are One. I cannot do to you, any more or less, than I can do to me. If you hurt, I am hurt; if you are happy, I too am happy.

AT THE SAME TIME, let there be a comfortable space between us; a space that allows for each of us to be our true and authentic Self; a space where we are both free to safely express who and what we really are. For although we are indeed One, we are not conjoined - we are both unique and separate Beings.

YOU, AND I, were created out of God's pure energy of Love. Pure Love is the energy of the Universe. You, and I, are no less than Living Gods; created in God's Loving Image.

Bazza

Barrie Frost is a mystic psychotherapist, who, in addition to his formal training in psychotherapy, has spent many years in the pursuit of spiritual enlightenment.

It is from this wide and varied background in life, that he has gleaned his extensive knowledge and understanding of life; both here on Planet Earth, and back home in the Spirit World.